Camping Journal

_____

_____

_____

Campground: _____   Dates: _____

Location: _____ Miles: _____
Time: _____ Cost: _____
Travel To Campground: _____ Weather: ☀ ⛅ ☁ 🌧 ⛈

INFORMATION:

Name: _____
Address: _____
Phone: _____
Site: _____
Site For Nest Time: _____
Cost: _____
Gps: _____
Rating: ★ ☆ ☆ ☆ ☆ ☆ ☆
Water Pressure: ★ ☆ ☆ ☆ ☆ ☆
Cleanliness: ★ ☆ ☆ ☆ ☆ ☆
Restrooms: ★ ☆ ☆ ☆ ☆ ☆

Amenities:

- ○ easy access
- ○ water
- ○ paved
- ○ 15 amp
- ○ shade
- ○ store
- ○ firewood
- ○ security
- ○ back-in
- ○ pet friendly
- ○ sewer
- ○ 30 amp
- ○ picnic table
- ○ tv
- ○ ice
- ○ pull-through
- ○ laundry
- ○ electricity
- ○ 50 amp
- ○ restrooms
- ○ fire ring
- ○ wifi
- ○ cafe
- ○ pool

Activites:

- ○ fishing
- ○ lake
- ○ fitness
- ○ shuffleboard
- ○ hiking
- ○ river
- ○ bike
- ○ pickleball
- ○ canoeing
- ○ hot tub
- ○ boat
- ○ golf

Camped With: _____
_____
_____
_____

New Friends: _____

_____

_____

Places Visited: _____

_____

_____

Drawing / Favorite Photo:

Notes:

_____

_____

_____

_____

_____

Campground: _____ Dates: _____

Location: _____ Miles: _____
Time: _____ Cost: _____
Travel To Campground: _____ Weather: ☀ ⛅ ☁ 🌧 ⛈

INFORMATION:

Name: _____	**Amenities:**	
Address: _____	○ easy access	○ picnic table
Phone: _____	○ water	○ tv
Site: _____	○ paved	○ ice
Site For Nest Time: _____	○ 15 amp	○ pull-through
Cost: _____	○ shade	○ laundry
Gps: _____	○ store	○ electricity
Rating: ★ ☆ ☆ ☆ ☆ ☆ ☆	○ firewood	○ 50 amp
Water Pressure: ★ ☆ ☆ ☆ ☆ ☆	○ security	○ restrooms
Cleanliness: ★ ☆ ☆ ☆ ☆ ☆	○ back-in	○ fire ring
Restrooms: ★ ☆ ☆ ☆ ☆ ☆	○ pet friendly	○ wifi
	○ sewer	○ cafe
	○ 30 amp	○ pool

Activites:

○ fishing	○ hiking	○ canoeing
○ lake	○ river	○ hot tub
○ fitness	○ bike	○ boat
○ shuffleboard	○ pickleball	○ golf

Camped With: _____
_____
_____
_____

New Friends: _____
_____
_____

Places Visited: _____
_____
_____

Drawing / Favorite Photo:

Notes:
_____
_____
_____
_____
_____

Campground: _____   Dates: _____

Location: _____   Miles: _____

Time: _____   Cost: _____

Travel To Campground: _____   Weather: ☀ 🌥 ⛅ 🌧 ⛈

INFORMATION:

Name: _____	**Amenities:**
Address: _____	○ easy access ○ picnic table
Phone: _____	○ water ○ tv
Site: _____	○ paved ○ ice
Site For Nest Time: _____	○ 15 amp ○ pull-through
Cost: _____	○ shade ○ laundry
Gps: _____	○ store ○ electricity
Rating: ★ ☆ ☆ ☆ ☆ ☆ ☆	○ firewood ○ 50 amp
Water Pressure: ★ ☆ ☆ ☆ ☆ ☆	○ security ○ restrooms
Cleanliness: ★ ☆ ☆ ☆ ☆ ☆	○ back-in ○ fire ring
Restrooms: ★ ☆ ☆ ☆ ☆ ☆	○ pet friendly ○ wifi
	○ sewer ○ cafe
	○ 30 amp ○ pool

Activites:

○ fishing	○ hiking	○ canoeing
○ lake	○ river	○ hot tub
○ fitness	○ bike	○ boat
○ shuffleboard	○ pickleball	○ golf

Camped With: _____
_____
_____
_____

New Friends: _____

_____

_____

Places Visited: _____

_____

_____

Drawing / Favorite Photo:

Notes:

_____

_____

_____

_____

_____

Campground: Dates:

Location: _____   Miles: _____

Time: _____   Cost: _____

Travel To Campground: _____   Weather: ☀ 🌤 ⛅ 🌧 ⛈

INFORMATION:

Name: _____	**Amenities:**
Address: _____	○ easy access ○ picnic table
Phone: _____	○ water ○ tv
Site: _____	○ paved ○ ice
Site For Nest Time: _____	○ 15 amp ○ pull-through
Cost: _____	○ shade ○ laundry
Gps: _____	○ store ○ electricity
Rating: ★ ☆ ☆ ☆ ☆ ☆ ☆	○ firewood ○ 50 amp
Water Pressure: ★ ☆ ☆ ☆ ☆ ☆	○ security ○ restrooms
Cleanliness: ★ ☆ ☆ ☆ ☆ ☆	○ back-in ○ fire ring
Restrooms: ★ ☆ ☆ ☆ ☆ ☆	○ pet friendly ○ wifi
	○ sewer ○ cafe
	○ 30 amp ○ pool

Activites:

○ fishing	○ hiking	○ canoeing
○ lake	○ river	○ hot tub
○ fitness	○ bike	○ boat
○ shuffleboard	○ pickleball	○ golf

Camped With: _____

_____

_____

_____

New Friends: _____

_____

_____

Places Visited: _____

_____

_____

Drawing / Favorite Photo:

Notes:

_____
_____
_____
_____
_____

Campground: Dates:

Location: _____ Miles: _____
Time: _____ Cost: _____
Travel To Campground: _____ Weather: ☀ ⛅ 🌤 🌧 ⛈

INFORMATION:

Name: _____	**Amenities:**
Address: _____	○ easy access ○ picnic table
Phone: _____	○ water ○ tv
Site: _____	○ paved ○ ice
Site For Nest Time: _____	○ 15 amp ○ pull-through
Cost: _____	○ shade ○ laundry
Gps: _____	○ store ○ electricity
Rating: ★ ☆ ☆ ☆ ☆ ☆ ☆	○ firewood ○ 50 amp
Water Pressure: ★ ☆ ☆ ☆ ☆ ☆	○ security ○ restrooms
Cleanliness: ★ ☆ ☆ ☆ ☆ ☆	○ back-in ○ fire ring
Restrooms: ★ ☆ ☆ ☆ ☆ ☆	○ pet friendly ○ wifi
	○ sewer ○ cafe
	○ 30 amp ○ pool

Activites:

○ fishing	○ hiking	○ canoeing
○ lake	○ river	○ hot tub
○ fitness	○ bike	○ boat
○ shuffleboard	○ pickleball	○ golf

Camped With: _____
_____
_____
_____

New Friends: _____
_____
_____

Places Visited: _____
_____
_____

Drawing / Favorite Photo:

Notes:
_____
_____
_____
_____
_____

Campground:

Dates:

Location: _____ Miles: _____

Time: _____ Cost: _____

Travel To Campground: _____ Weather: ☀ ⛅ ☁ 🌧 ⛈

INFORMATION:

Name: _____	**Amenities:**
Address: _____	○ easy access ○ picnic table
Phone: _____	○ water ○ tv
Site: _____	○ paved ○ ice
Site For Nest Time: _____	○ 15 amp ○ pull-through
Cost: _____	○ shade ○ laundry
Gps: _____	○ store ○ electricity
Rating: ★ ☆ ☆ ☆ ☆ ☆ ☆	○ firewood ○ 50 amp
Water Pressure: ★ ☆ ☆ ☆ ☆ ☆	○ security ○ restrooms
Cleanliness: ★ ☆ ☆ ☆ ☆ ☆ ☆	○ back-in ○ fire ring
Restrooms: ★ ☆ ☆ ☆ ☆ ☆ ☆	○ pet friendly ○ wifi
	○ sewer ○ cafe
	○ 30 amp ○ pool

Activites:

○ fishing   ○ hiking   ○ canoeing
○ lake   ○ river   ○ hot tub
○ fitness   ○ bike   ○ boat
○ shuffleboard   ○ pickleball   ○ golf

Camped With: _____

_____

_____

_____

New Friends: _____
_____
_____

Places Visited: _____
_____
_____

Drawing / Favorite Photo:

Notes:
_____
_____
_____
_____
_____

Campground: _____ Dates: _____

Location: _____ Miles: _____
Time: _____ Cost: _____
Travel To Campground: _____ Weather: ☀ ⛅ ☁ 🌧 ⛈

INFORMATION:

Name: _____	**Amenities:**
Address: _____	○ easy access ○ picnic table
Phone: _____	○ water ○ tv
Site: _____	○ paved ○ ice
Site For Nest Time: _____	○ 15 amp ○ pull-through
Cost: _____	○ shade ○ laundry
Gps: _____	○ store ○ electricity
Rating: ★ ☆ ☆ ☆ ☆ ☆ ☆	○ firewood ○ 50 amp
Water Pressure: ★ ☆ ☆ ☆ ☆ ☆	○ security ○ restrooms
Cleanliness: ★ ☆ ☆ ☆ ☆ ☆	○ back-in ○ fire ring
Restrooms: ★ ☆ ☆ ☆ ☆ ☆	○ pet friendly ○ wifi
	○ sewer ○ cafe
	○ 30 amp ○ pool

Activites:

○ fishing	○ hiking	○ canoeing
○ lake	○ river	○ hot tub
○ fitness	○ bike	○ boat
○ shuffleboard	○ pickleball	○ golf

Camped With: _____
_____
_____
_____

New Friends: _____

_____

_____

Places Visited: _____

_____

_____

Drawing / Favorite Photo:

Notes:

_____

_____

_____

_____

Campground: _____   Dates: _____

Location: _____   Miles: _____
Time: _____   Cost: _____
Travel To Campground: _____   Weather: ☀ ⛅ ☁ 🌧 ⛈

INFORMATION:

Name: _____	**Amenities:**
Address: _____	○ easy access ○ picnic table
Phone: _____	○ water ○ tv
Site: _____	○ paved ○ ice
Site For Nest Time: _____	○ 15 amp ○ pull-through
Cost: _____	○ shade ○ laundry
Gps: _____	○ store ○ electricity
Rating: ★ ☆ ☆ ☆ ☆ ☆ ☆	○ firewood ○ 50 amp
Water Pressure: ★ ☆ ☆ ☆ ☆ ☆	○ security ○ restrooms
Cleanliness: ★ ☆ ☆ ☆ ☆ ☆	○ back-in ○ fire ring
Restrooms: ★ ☆ ☆ ☆ ☆ ☆	○ pet friendly ○ wifi
	○ sewer ○ cafe
	○ 30 amp ○ pool

Activites:

○ fishing   ○ hiking   ○ canoeing
○ lake   ○ river   ○ hot tub
○ fitness   ○ bike   ○ boat
○ shuffleboard ○ pickleball   ○ golf

Camped With: _____
_____
_____
_____

New Friends: _____
_____
_____

Places Visited: _____
_____
_____

Drawing / Favorite Photo:

Notes:
_____
_____
_____
_____
_____

Campground: _____   Dates: _____

Location: _____   Miles: _____

Time: _____   Cost: _____

Travel To Campground: _____   Weather: ☀ ⛅ ☁ 🌧 ⛈

INFORMATION:

Name: _____	**Amenities:**
Address: _____	○ easy access ○ picnic table
Phone: _____	○ water ○ tv
Site: _____	○ paved ○ ice
Site For Nest Time: _____	○ 15 amp ○ pull-through
Cost: _____	○ shade ○ laundry
Gps: _____	○ store ○ electricity
Rating: ★ ☆ ☆ ☆ ☆ ☆ ☆	○ firewood ○ 50 amp
Water Pressure: ★ ☆ ☆ ☆ ☆ ☆	○ security ○ restrooms
Cleanliness: ★ ☆ ☆ ☆ ☆ ☆	○ back-in ○ fire ring
Restrooms: ★ ☆ ☆ ☆ ☆ ☆	○ pet friendly ○ wifi
	○ sewer ○ cafe
	○ 30 amp ○ pool

Activites:

○ fishing	○ hiking	○ canoeing
○ lake	○ river	○ hot tub
○ fitness	○ bike	○ boat
○ shuffleboard	○ pickleball	○ golf

Camped With: _____

_____

_____

_____

New Friends: _____
_____
_____

Places Visited: _____
_____
_____

Drawing / Favorite Photo:

Notes:
_____
_____
_____
_____
_____
_____

Campground: _____   Dates: _____

Location: _____   Miles: _____
Time: _____   Cost: _____
Travel To Campground: _____   Weather: ☀ 🌦 ⛅ 🌧 ⛈

INFORMATION:

Name: _____	**Amenities:**
Address: _____	○ easy access ○ picnic table
Phone: _____	○ water ○ tv
Site: _____	○ paved ○ ice
Site For Nest Time: _____	○ 15 amp ○ pull-through
Cost: _____	○ shade ○ laundry
Gps: _____	○ store ○ electricity
Rating: ★ ☆ ☆ ☆ ☆ ☆ ☆	○ firewood ○ 50 amp
Water Pressure: ★ ☆ ☆ ☆ ☆ ☆	○ security ○ restrooms
Cleanliness: ★ ☆ ☆ ☆ ☆ ☆ ☆	○ back-in ○ fire ring
Restrooms: ★ ☆ ☆ ☆ ☆ ☆ ☆	○ pet friendly ○ wifi
	○ sewer ○ cafe
	○ 30 amp ○ pool

Activites:

○ fishing   ○ hiking   ○ canoeing
○ lake   ○ river   ○ hot tub
○ fitness   ○ bike   ○ boat
○ shuffleboard   ○ pickleball   ○ golf

Camped With: _____
_____
_____
_____

New Friends: _____
_____
_____

Places Visited: _____
_____
_____

Drawing / Favorite Photo:

Notes:
_____
_____
_____
_____
_____

Campground: _____

Dates: _____

Location: _____ Miles: _____

Time: _____ Cost: _____

Travel To Campground: _____ Weather: ☀ ⛅ ☁ 🌧 ⛈

INFORMATION:

Name: _____	**Amenities:**
Address: _____	○ easy access ○ picnic table
Phone: _____	○ water ○ tv
Site: _____	○ paved ○ ice
Site For Nest Time: _____	○ 15 amp ○ pull-through
Cost: _____	○ shade ○ laundry
Gps: _____	○ store ○ electricity
Rating: ★ ☆ ☆ ☆ ☆ ☆ ☆	○ firewood ○ 50 amp
Water Pressure: ★ ☆ ☆ ☆ ☆ ☆	○ security ○ restrooms
Cleanliness: ★ ☆ ☆ ☆ ☆ ☆ ☆	○ back-in ○ fire ring
Restrooms: ★ ☆ ☆ ☆ ☆ ☆ ☆	○ pet friendly ○ wifi
	○ sewer ○ cafe
	○ 30 amp ○ pool

Activites:

○ fishing	○ hiking	○ canoeing
○ lake	○ river	○ hot tub
○ fitness	○ bike	○ boat
○ shuffleboard	○ pickleball	○ golf

Camped With: _____

_____

_____

_____

New Friends: _____
_____
_____

Places Visited: _____
_____
_____

Drawing / Favorite Photo:

Notes:
_____
_____
_____
_____
_____

Campground: _____   Dates: _____

Location: _____   Miles: _____
Time: _____   Cost: _____
Travel To Campground: _____   Weather: ☀ ⛅ ☁ 🌧 ⛈

INFORMATION:

Name: _____
Address: _____
Phone: _____
Site: _____
Site For Nest Time: _____
Cost: _____
Gps: _____
Rating: ★ ☆ ☆ ☆ ☆ ☆ ☆
Water Pressure: ★ ☆ ☆ ☆ ☆ ☆
Cleanliness: ★ ☆ ☆ ☆ ☆ ☆
Restrooms: ★ ☆ ☆ ☆ ☆ ☆

Amenities:
- ○ easy access
- ○ water
- ○ paved
- ○ 15 amp
- ○ shade
- ○ store
- ○ firewood
- ○ security
- ○ back-in
- ○ pet friendly
- ○ sewer
- ○ 30 amp
- ○ picnic table
- ○ tv
- ○ ice
- ○ pull-through
- ○ laundry
- ○ electricity
- ○ 50 amp
- ○ restrooms
- ○ fire ring
- ○ wifi
- ○ cafe
- ○ pool

Activites:

- ○ fishing
- ○ lake
- ○ fitness
- ○ shuffleboard
- ○ hiking
- ○ river
- ○ bike
- ○ pickleball
- ○ canoeing
- ○ hot tub
- ○ boat
- ○ golf

Camped With: _____
_____
_____
_____

New Friends: _____

_____

_____

Places Visited: _____

_____

_____

Drawing / Favorite Photo:

Notes:

Campground:

Dates:

Location: _____ Miles: _____

Time: _____ Cost: _____

Travel To Campground: _____ Weather: ☀ ⛅ ☁ 🌧 ⛈

INFORMATION:

Name: _____	**Amenities:**
Address: _____	○ easy access ○ picnic table
Phone: _____	○ water ○ tv
Site: _____	○ paved ○ ice
Site For Nest Time: _____	○ 15 amp ○ pull-through
Cost: _____	○ shade ○ laundry
Gps: _____	○ store ○ electricity
Rating: ★ ☆ ☆ ☆ ☆ ☆ ☆	○ firewood ○ 50 amp
Water Pressure: ★ ☆ ☆ ☆ ☆ ☆	○ security ○ restrooms
Cleanliness: ★ ☆ ☆ ☆ ☆ ☆	○ back-in ○ fire ring
Restrooms: ★ ☆ ☆ ☆ ☆ ☆	○ pet friendly ○ wifi
	○ sewer ○ cafe
	○ 30 amp ○ pool

Activites:

○ fishing	○ hiking	○ canoeing
○ lake	○ river	○ hot tub
○ fitness	○ bike	○ boat
○ shuffleboard	○ pickleball	○ golf

Camped With: _____

_____

_____

New Friends: _____

_____
_____

Places Visited: _____

_____
_____

Drawing / Favorite Photo:

Notes:

_____
_____
_____
_____
_____

Campground: _____ Dates: _____

Location: _____ Miles: _____

Time: _____ Cost: _____

Travel To Campground: _____ Weather: ☀ ❄ ⛅ 🌧 ⛈

INFORMATION:

Name: _____	**Amenities:**
Address: _____	○ easy access ○ picnic table
Phone: _____	○ water ○ tv
Site: _____	○ paved ○ ice
Site For Nest Time: _____	○ 15 amp ○ pull-through
Cost: _____	○ shade ○ laundry
Gps: _____	○ store ○ electricity
Rating: ★ ☆ ☆ ☆ ☆ ☆ ☆	○ firewood ○ 50 amp
Water Pressure: ★ ☆ ☆ ☆ ☆ ☆	○ security ○ restrooms
Cleanliness: ★ ☆ ☆ ☆ ☆ ☆	○ back-in ○ fire ring
Restrooms: ★ ☆ ☆ ☆ ☆ ☆ ☆	○ pet friendly ○ wifi
	○ sewer ○ cafe
	○ 30 amp ○ pool

Activites:

○ fishing   ○ hiking   ○ canoeing
○ lake   ○ river   ○ hot tub
○ fitness   ○ bike   ○ boat
○ shuffleboard   ○ pickleball   ○ golf

Camped With: _____

_____

_____

New Friends: _____
_____
_____

Places Visited: _____
_____
_____

Drawing / Favorite Photo:

Notes:
_____
_____
_____
_____
_____

Campground: _____ # Dates: _____

Location: _____   Miles: _____
Time: _____   Cost: _____
Travel To Campground: _____   Weather: ☀ ⛅ ☁ 🌧 ⛈

INFORMATION:

Name: _____	**Amenities:**
Address: _____	○ easy access ○ picnic table
Phone: _____	○ water ○ tv
Site: _____	○ paved ○ ice
Site For Nest Time: _____	○ 15 amp ○ pull-through
Cost: _____	○ shade ○ laundry
Gps: _____	○ store ○ electricity
Rating: ★ ☆ ☆ ☆ ☆ ☆ ☆	○ firewood ○ 50 amp
Water Pressure: ★ ☆ ☆ ☆ ☆ ☆	○ security ○ restrooms
Cleanliness: ★ ☆ ☆ ☆ ☆ ☆	○ back-in ○ fire ring
Restrooms: ★ ☆ ☆ ☆ ☆ ☆	○ pet friendly ○ wifi
	○ sewer ○ cafe
	○ 30 amp ○ pool

Activites:

○ fishing	○ hiking	○ canoeing
○ lake	○ river	○ hot tub
○ fitness	○ bike	○ boat
○ shuffleboard	○ pickleball	○ golf

Camped With: _____
_____
_____
_____

New Friends: _____
_____
_____

Places Visited: _____
_____
_____

Drawing / Favorite Photo:

Notes:
_____
_____
_____
_____
_____

Campground: _____   Dates: _____

Location: _____ Miles: _____
Time: _____ Cost: _____
Travel To Campground: _____ Weather: ☀ ⛅ ☁ 🌧 ⛈

INFORMATION:

Name: _____	**Amenities:**
Address: _____	○ easy access ○ picnic table
Phone: _____	○ water ○ tv
Site: _____	○ paved ○ ice
Site For Nest Time: _____	○ 15 amp ○ pull-through
Cost: _____	○ shade ○ laundry
Gps: _____	○ store ○ electricity
Rating: ★ ☆ ☆ ☆ ☆ ☆ ☆	○ firewood ○ 50 amp
Water Pressure: ★ ☆ ☆ ☆ ☆	○ security ○ restrooms
Cleanliness: ★ ☆ ☆ ☆ ☆ ☆	○ back-in ○ fire ring
Restrooms: ★ ☆ ☆ ☆ ☆ ☆	○ pet friendly ○ wifi
	○ sewer ○ cafe
	○ 30 amp ○ pool

Activites:

○ fishing   ○ hiking   ○ canoeing
○ lake   ○ river   ○ hot tub
○ fitness   ○ bike   ○ boat
○ shuffleboard ○ pickleball ○ golf

Camped With: _____
_____
_____
_____

New Friends: _____

_____

_____

Places Visited: _____

_____

_____

Drawing / Favorite Photo:

Notes:

_____

_____

_____

_____

_____

Campground: _____   Dates: _____

Location: _____   Miles: _____
Time: _____   Cost: _____
Travel To Campground: _____   Weather: ☀ ⛅ ☁ 🌧 ⛈

INFORMATION:

Name: _____	**Amenities:**
Address: _____	○ easy access ○ picnic table
Phone: _____	○ water ○ tv
Site: _____	○ paved ○ ice
Site For Nest Time: _____	○ 15 amp ○ pull-through
Cost: _____	○ shade ○ laundry
Gps: _____	○ store ○ electricity
Rating: ★ ☆ ☆ ☆ ☆ ☆ ☆	○ firewood ○ 50 amp
Water Pressure: ★ ☆ ☆ ☆ ☆ ☆	○ security ○ restrooms
Cleanliness: ★ ☆ ☆ ☆ ☆ ☆	○ back-in ○ fire ring
Restrooms: ★ ☆ ☆ ☆ ☆ ☆	○ pet friendly ○ wifi
	○ sewer ○ cafe
	○ 30 amp ○ pool

Activites:

○ fishing   ○ hiking   ○ canoeing
○ lake   ○ river   ○ hot tub
○ fitness   ○ bike   ○ boat
○ shuffleboard   ○ pickleball   ○ golf

Camped With: _____
_____
_____
_____

New Friends: _____
_____
_____

Places Visited: _____
_____
_____

Drawing / Favorite Photo:

Notes:
_____
_____
_____
_____
_____

Campground: _____ Dates: _____

Location: _____   Miles: _____
Time: _____   Cost: _____
Travel To Campground: _____   Weather: ☀ ⛅ ☁ 🌧 ⛈

INFORMATION:

Name: _____	**Amenities:**
Address: _____	○ easy access ○ picnic table
Phone: _____	○ water ○ tv
Site: _____	○ paved ○ ice
Site For Nest Time: _____	○ 15 amp ○ pull-through
Cost: _____	○ shade ○ laundry
Gps: _____	○ store ○ electricity
Rating: ★ ☆ ☆ ☆ ☆ ☆ ☆	○ firewood ○ 50 amp
Water Pressure: ★ ☆ ☆ ☆ ☆ ☆	○ security ○ restrooms
Cleanliness: ★ ☆ ☆ ☆ ☆ ☆	○ back-in ○ fire ring
Restrooms: ★ ☆ ☆ ☆ ☆ ☆	○ pet friendly ○ wifi
	○ sewer ○ cafe
	○ 30 amp ○ pool

Activites:

○ fishing   ○ hiking   ○ canoeing
○ lake   ○ river   ○ hot tub
○ fitness   ○ bike   ○ boat
○ shuffleboard   ○ pickleball   ○ golf

Camped With: _____
_____
_____
_____

New Friends: _____
_____
_____

Places Visited: _____
_____
_____

Drawing / Favorite Photo:

Notes:
_____
_____
_____
_____
_____

Campground: _____ Dates: _____

Location: _____ Miles: _____
Time: _____ Cost: _____
Travel To Campground: _____ Weather: ☀ ⛅ ☁ 🌧 ⛈

INFORMATION:

Name: _____	**Amenities:**
Address: _____	○ easy access ○ picnic table
Phone: _____	○ water ○ tv
Site: _____	○ paved ○ ice
Site For Nest Time: _____	○ 15 amp ○ pull-through
Cost: _____	○ shade ○ laundry
Gps: _____	○ store ○ electricity
Rating: ★ ☆ ☆ ☆ ☆ ☆ ☆	○ firewood ○ 50 amp
Water Pressure: ★ ☆ ☆ ☆ ☆ ☆	○ security ○ restrooms
Cleanliness: ★ ☆ ☆ ☆ ☆ ☆	○ back-in ○ fire ring
Restrooms: ★ ☆ ☆ ☆ ☆ ☆	○ pet friendly ○ wifi
	○ sewer ○ cafe
	○ 30 amp ○ pool

Activites:

○ fishing	○ hiking	○ canoeing
○ lake	○ river	○ hot tub
○ fitness	○ bike	○ boat
○ shuffleboard	○ pickleball	○ golf

Camped With: _____
_____
_____
_____

New Friends: _____
_____
_____ _____

Places Visited: _____
_____
_____

Drawing / Favorite Photo:

Notes:
_____
_____
_____
_____
_____

Campground: Dates:

Location: _____   Miles: _____
Time: _____   Cost: _____
Travel To Campground: _____   Weather: ☀ ⛅ ☁ 🌧 ⛈

INFORMATION:

Name: _____	**Amenities:**
Address: _____	○ easy access ○ picnic table
Phone: _____	○ water ○ tv
Site: _____	○ paved ○ ice
Site For Nest Time: _____	○ 15 amp ○ pull-through
Cost: _____	○ shade ○ laundry
Gps: _____	○ store ○ electricity
Rating: ★ ☆ ☆ ☆ ☆ ☆ ☆	○ firewood ○ 50 amp
Water Pressure: ★ ☆ ☆ ☆ ☆ ☆	○ security ○ restrooms
Cleanliness: ★ ☆ ☆ ☆ ☆ ☆ ☆	○ back-in ○ fire ring
Restrooms: ★ ☆ ☆ ☆ ☆ ☆ ☆	○ pet friendly ○ wifi
	○ sewer ○ cafe
	○ 30 amp ○ pool

Activites:

○ fishing   ○ hiking   ○ canoeing
○ lake   ○ river   ○ hot tub
○ fitness   ○ bike   ○ boat
○ shuffleboard   ○ pickleball   ○ golf

Camped With: _____
_____
_____
_____

New Friends: _____

_____

_____

Places Visited: _____

_____

_____

Drawing / Favorite Photo:

Notes:

_____

_____

_____

_____

_____

Campground: _____ Dates: _____

Location: _____ Miles: _____

Time: _____ Cost: _____

Travel To Campground: _____ Weather: ☀ ⛅ ☁ 🌧 ⛈

INFORMATION:

Name: _____

Address: _____

Phone: _____

Site: _____

Site For Nest Time: _____

Cost: _____

Gps: _____

Rating: ★ ☆ ☆ ☆ ☆ ☆ ☆

Water Pressure: ★ ☆ ☆ ☆ ☆ ☆

Cleanliness: ★ ☆ ☆ ☆ ☆ ☆

Restrooms: ★ ☆ ☆ ☆ ☆ ☆

Amenities:

- ○ easy access
- ○ water
- ○ paved
- ○ 15 amp
- ○ shade
- ○ store
- ○ firewood
- ○ security
- ○ back-in
- ○ pet friendly
- ○ sewer
- ○ 30 amp

- ○ picnic table
- ○ tv
- ○ ice
- ○ pull-through
- ○ laundry
- ○ electricity
- ○ 50 amp
- ○ restrooms
- ○ fire ring
- ○ wifi
- ○ cafe
- ○ pool

Activites:

- ○ fishing
- ○ lake
- ○ fitness
- ○ shuffleboard

- ○ hiking
- ○ river
- ○ bike
- ○ pickleball

- ○ canoeing
- ○ hot tub
- ○ boat
- ○ golf

Camped With: _____

_____

_____

New Friends: _____
_____
_____

Places Visited: _____
_____
_____

Drawing / Favorite Photo:

Notes:
_____
_____
_____
_____
_____

Campground: _____   Dates: _____

Location: _____   Miles: _____
Time: _____   Cost: _____
Travel To Campground: _____   Weather: ☀ 🌤 ⛅ 🌧 ⛈

INFORMATION:

Name: _____	**Amenities:**
Address: _____	○ easy access ○ picnic table
Phone: _____	○ water ○ tv
Site: _____	○ paved ○ ice
Site For Nest Time: _____	○ 15 amp ○ pull-through
Cost: _____	○ shade ○ laundry
Gps: _____	○ store ○ electricity
Rating: ★ ☆ ☆ ☆ ☆ ☆ ☆	○ firewood ○ 50 amp
Water Pressure: ★ ☆ ☆ ☆ ☆ ☆	○ security ○ restrooms
Cleanliness: ★ ☆ ☆ ☆ ☆ ☆	○ back-in ○ fire ring
Restrooms: ★ ☆ ☆ ☆ ☆ ☆	○ pet friendly ○ wifi
	○ sewer ○ cafe
	○ 30 amp ○ pool

Activites:

○ fishing   ○ hiking   ○ canoeing
○ lake   ○ river   ○ hot tub
○ fitness   ○ bike   ○ boat
○ shuffleboard   ○ pickleball   ○ golf

Camped With: _____
_____
_____
_____

New Friends: _____

_____

_____

Places Visited: _____

_____

_____

Drawing / Favorite Photo:

Notes:

_____

_____

_____

_____

Campground: _____   Dates: _____

Location: _____   Miles: _____

Time: _____   Cost: _____

Travel To Campground: _____   Weather: ☀ ⛅ ☁ 🌧 ⛈

INFORMATION:

Name: _____

Address: _____

Phone: _____

Site: _____

Site For Nest Time: _____

Cost: _____

Gps: _____

Rating: ★ ☆ ☆ ☆ ☆ ☆ ☆

Water Pressure: ★ ☆ ☆ ☆ ☆ ☆

Cleanliness: ★ ☆ ☆ ☆ ☆ ☆

Restrooms: ★ ☆ ☆ ☆ ☆ ☆

Amenities:

- ○ easy access
- ○ water
- ○ paved
- ○ 15 amp
- ○ shade
- ○ store
- ○ firewood
- ○ security
- ○ back-in
- ○ pet friendly
- ○ sewer
- ○ 30 amp
- ○ picnic table
- ○ tv
- ○ ice
- ○ pull-through
- ○ laundry
- ○ electricity
- ○ 50 amp
- ○ restrooms
- ○ fire ring
- ○ wifi
- ○ cafe
- ○ pool

Activites:

- ○ fishing
- ○ lake
- ○ fitness
- ○ shuffleboard
- ○ hiking
- ○ river
- ○ bike
- ○ pickleball
- ○ canoeing
- ○ hot tub
- ○ boat
- ○ golf

Camped With: _____

_____

_____

New Friends: _____

_____

_____

Places Visited: _____

_____

_____

Drawing / Favorite Photo:

Notes:

_____
_____
_____
_____
_____

Campground: _____   Dates: _____

Location: _____   Miles: _____

Time: _____   Cost: _____

Travel To Campground: _____   Weather: ☀ ⛅ ☁ 🌧 ⛈

INFORMATION:

Name: _____	**Amenities:**
Address: _____	○ easy access ○ picnic table
Phone: _____	○ water ○ tv
Site: _____	○ paved ○ ice
Site For Nest Time: _____	○ 15 amp ○ pull-through
Cost: _____	○ shade ○ laundry
Gps: _____	○ store ○ electricity
Rating: ★ ☆ ☆ ☆ ☆ ☆ ☆	○ firewood ○ 50 amp
Water Pressure: ★ ☆ ☆ ☆ ☆ ☆	○ security ○ restrooms
Cleanliness: ★ ☆ ☆ ☆ ☆ ☆	○ back-in ○ fire ring
Restrooms: ★ ☆ ☆ ☆ ☆ ☆	○ pet friendly ○ wifi
	○ sewer ○ cafe
	○ 30 amp ○ pool

Activites:

○ fishing   ○ hiking   ○ canoeing
○ lake   ○ river   ○ hot tub
○ fitness   ○ bike   ○ boat
○ shuffleboard   ○ pickleball   ○ golf

Camped With: _____
_____
_____
_____

New Friends: _____

_____
_____

Places Visited: _____

_____
_____

Drawing / Favorite Photo:

Notes:

_____
_____
_____
_____
_____

Campground: _____ Dates: _____

Location: _____ Miles: _____

Time: _____ Cost: _____

Travel To Campground: _____ Weather: ☀ ⛅ ☁ 🌧 ⛈

INFORMATION:

Name: _____	**Amenities:**
Address: _____	
Phone: _____	○ easy access ○ picnic table
Site: _____	○ water ○ tv
Site For Nest Time: _____	○ paved ○ ice
Cost: _____	○ 15 amp ○ pull-through
Gps: _____	○ shade ○ laundry
Rating: ★ ☆ ☆ ☆ ☆ ☆ ☆	○ store ○ electricity
Water Pressure: ★ ☆ ☆ ☆ ☆ ☆	○ firewood ○ 50 amp
Cleanliness: ★ ☆ ☆ ☆ ☆ ☆	○ security ○ restrooms
Restrooms: ★ ☆ ☆ ☆ ☆ ☆ ☆	○ back-in ○ fire ring
	○ pet friendly ○ wifi
	○ sewer ○ cafe
	○ 30 amp ○ pool

Activites:

○ fishing   ○ hiking   ○ canoeing
○ lake   ○ river   ○ hot tub
○ fitness   ○ bike   ○ boat
○ shuffleboard   ○ pickleball   ○ golf

Camped With: _____

_____

_____

New Friends: _____
_____
_____

Places Visited: _____
_____
_____

Drawing / Favorite Photo:

Notes:
_____
_____
_____
_____
_____
_____

Campground: _____   Dates: _____

Location: _____   Miles: _____
Time: _____   Cost: _____
Travel To Campground: _____   Weather: ☀ ⛅ ☁ 🌧 ⛈

INFORMATION:

Name: _____	**Amenities:**
Address: _____	○ easy access ○ picnic table
Phone: _____	○ water ○ tv
Site: _____	○ paved ○ ice
Site For Nest Time: _____	○ 15 amp ○ pull-through
Cost: _____	○ shade ○ laundry
Gps: _____	○ store ○ electricity
Rating: ★ ☆ ☆ ☆ ☆ ☆ ☆	○ firewood ○ 50 amp
Water Pressure: ★ ☆ ☆ ☆ ☆ ☆	○ security ○ restrooms
Cleanliness: ★ ☆ ☆ ☆ ☆ ☆	○ back-in ○ fire ring
Restrooms: ★ ☆ ☆ ☆ ☆ ☆	○ pet friendly ○ wifi
	○ sewer ○ cafe
	○ 30 amp ○ pool

Activites:

○ fishing	○ hiking	○ canoeing
○ lake	○ river	○ hot tub
○ fitness	○ bike	○ boat
○ shuffleboard	○ pickleball	○ golf

Camped With: _____
_____
_____
_____

New Friends: _____

_____

_____

Places Visited: _____

_____

_____

Drawing / Favorite Photo:

Notes:

Campground:

Dates:

Location: _____ Miles: _____

Time: _____ Cost: _____

Travel To Campground: _____ Weather: ☀ ⛅ ⛅ ☁ 🌧

INFORMATION:

Name: _____	**Amenities:**
Address: _____	○ easy access ○ picnic table
Phone: _____	○ water ○ tv
Site: _____	○ paved ○ ice
Site For Nest Time: _____	○ 15 amp ○ pull-through
Cost: _____	○ shade ○ laundry
Gps: _____	○ store ○ electricity
Rating: ★ ☆ ☆ ☆ ☆ ☆ ☆	○ firewood ○ 50 amp
Water Pressure: ★ ☆ ☆ ☆ ☆ ☆	○ security ○ restrooms
Cleanliness: ★ ☆ ☆ ☆ ☆ ☆	○ back-in ○ fire ring
Restrooms: ★ ☆ ☆ ☆ ☆ ☆	○ pet friendly ○ wifi
	○ sewer ○ cafe
	○ 30 amp ○ pool

Activites:

○ fishing   ○ hiking   ○ canoeing
○ lake   ○ river   ○ hot tub
○ fitness   ○ bike   ○ boat
○ shuffleboard   ○ pickleball   ○ golf

Camped With: _____
_____
_____
_____

New Friends: _____

_____

_____

Places Visited: _____

_____

_____

Drawing / Favorite Photo:

Notes:

_____
_____
_____
_____
_____

Campground:

Dates:

Location: _____ Miles: _____

Time: _____ Cost: _____

Travel To Campground: _____ Weather: ☀ ⛅ 🌤 ☁ 🌧

INFORMATION:

Name: _____

Address: _____

Phone: _____

Site: _____

Site For Nest Time: _____

Cost: _____

Gps: _____

Rating: ★ ☆ ☆ ☆ ☆ ☆ ☆

Water Pressure: ★ ☆ ☆ ☆ ☆ ☆

Cleanliness: ★ ☆ ☆ ☆ ☆ ☆ ☆

Restrooms: ★ ☆ ☆ ☆ ☆ ☆ ☆

Amenities:

- ○ easy access
- ○ water
- ○ paved
- ○ 15 amp
- ○ shade
- ○ store
- ○ firewood
- ○ security
- ○ back-in
- ○ pet friendly
- ○ sewer
- ○ 30 amp
- ○ picnic table
- ○ tv
- ○ ice
- ○ pull-through
- ○ laundry
- ○ electricity
- ○ 50 amp
- ○ restrooms
- ○ fire ring
- ○ wifi
- ○ cafe
- ○ pool

Activites:

- ○ fishing
- ○ lake
- ○ fitness
- ○ shuffleboard
- ○ hiking
- ○ river
- ○ bike
- ○ pickleball
- ○ canoeing
- ○ hot tub
- ○ boat
- ○ golf

Camped With: _____

_____

_____

New Friends: _____

_____

_____

Places Visited: _____

_____

_____

Drawing / Favorite Photo:

Notes:

Campground:

Dates:

Location: _____ Miles: _____

Time: _____ Cost: _____

Travel To Campground: _____ Weather: ☀ ⛅ ⛆ ☁ ⛈

INFORMATION:

Name: _____

Address: _____

Phone: _____

Site: _____

Site For Nest Time: _____

Cost: _____

Gps: _____

Rating: ★ ☆ ☆ ☆ ☆ ☆ ☆

Water Pressure: ★ ☆ ☆ ☆ ☆ ☆

Cleanliness: ★ ☆ ☆ ☆ ☆ ☆

Restrooms: ★ ☆ ☆ ☆ ☆ ☆

Amenities:

- ○ easy access ○ picnic table
- ○ water   ○ tv
- ○ paved   ○ ice
- ○ 15 amp   ○ pull-through
- ○ shade   ○ laundry
- ○ store   ○ electricity
- ○ firewood   ○ 50 amp
- ○ security   ○ restrooms
- ○ back-in   ○ fire ring
- ○ pet friendly ○ wifi
- ○ sewer   ○ cafe
- ○ 30 amp   ○ pool

Activites:

- ○ fishing   ○ hiking   ○ canoeing
- ○ lake   ○ river   ○ hot tub
- ○ fitness   ○ bike   ○ boat
- ○ shuffleboard ○ pickleball   ○ golf

Camped With: _____

_____

_____

New Friends: _____

_____

_____

Places Visited: _____

_____

_____

Drawing / Favorite Photo:

Notes:

_____
_____
_____
_____
_____
_____

Campground: _____

Dates: _____

Location: _____ Miles: _____

Time: _____ Cost: _____

Travel To Campground: _____ Weather: ☀ ⛅ ☁ 🌧 ⛈

INFORMATION:

Name: _____	**Amenities:**
Address: _____	○ easy access ○ picnic table
Phone: _____	○ water ○ tv
Site: _____	○ paved ○ ice
Site For Nest Time: _____	○ 15 amp ○ pull-through
Cost: _____	○ shade ○ laundry
Gps: _____	○ store ○ electricity
Rating: ★ ☆ ☆ ☆ ☆ ☆ ☆	○ firewood ○ 50 amp
Water Pressure: ★ ☆ ☆ ☆ ☆ ☆	○ security ○ restrooms
Cleanliness: ★ ☆ ☆ ☆ ☆ ☆ ☆	○ back-in ○ fire ring
Restrooms: ★ ☆ ☆ ☆ ☆ ☆ ☆	○ pet friendly ○ wifi
	○ sewer ○ cafe
	○ 30 amp ○ pool

Activites:

○ fishing	○ hiking	○ canoeing
○ lake	○ river	○ hot tub
○ fitness	○ bike	○ boat
○ shuffleboard	○ pickleball	○ golf

Camped With: _____
_____
_____

New Friends: _____
_____
_____

Places Visited: _____
_____
_____

Drawing / Favorite Photo:

Notes:
_____
_____
_____
_____
_____

Campground: Dates:

Location: _____ Miles: _____

Time: _____ Cost: _____

Travel To Campground: _____ Weather: ☀ ⛅ ☁ 🌧 ⛈

INFORMATION:

Name: _____

Address: _____

Phone: _____

Site: _____

Site For Nest Time: _____

Cost: _____

Gps: _____

Rating: ★ ☆ ☆ ☆ ☆ ☆ ☆

Water Pressure: ★ ☆ ☆ ☆ ☆ ☆

Cleanliness: ★ ☆ ☆ ☆ ☆ ☆ ☆

Restrooms: ★ ☆ ☆ ☆ ☆ ☆ ☆

Amenities:

- ○ easy access
- ○ water
- ○ paved
- ○ 15 amp
- ○ shade
- ○ store
- ○ firewood
- ○ security
- ○ back-in
- ○ pet friendly
- ○ sewer
- ○ 30 amp

- ○ picnic table
- ○ tv
- ○ ice
- ○ pull-through
- ○ laundry
- ○ electricity
- ○ 50 amp
- ○ restrooms
- ○ fire ring
- ○ wifi
- ○ cafe
- ○ pool

Activites:

- ○ fishing
- ○ lake
- ○ fitness
- ○ shuffleboard

- ○ hiking
- ○ river
- ○ bike
- ○ pickleball

- ○ canoeing
- ○ hot tub
- ○ boat
- ○ golf

Camped With: _____

_____

_____

New Friends: _____
_____
_____

Places Visited: _____
_____
_____

Drawing / Favorite Photo:

Notes:
_____
_____
_____
_____
_____

Campground: _____ Dates: _____

Location: _____ Miles: _____

Time: _____ Cost: _____

Travel To Campground: _____ Weather: ☀ ⛅ ☁ 🌧 ⛈

INFORMATION:

Name: _____

Address: _____

Phone: _____

Site: _____

Site For Nest Time: _____

Cost: _____

Gps: _____

Rating: ★ ☆ ☆ ☆ ☆ ☆ ☆

Water Pressure: ★ ☆ ☆ ☆ ☆ ☆

Cleanliness: ★ ☆ ☆ ☆ ☆ ☆

Restrooms: ★ ☆ ☆ ☆ ☆ ☆

Amenities:

- ○ easy access
- ○ water
- ○ paved
- ○ 15 amp
- ○ shade
- ○ store
- ○ firewood
- ○ security
- ○ back-in
- ○ pet friendly
- ○ sewer
- ○ 30 amp
- ○ picnic table
- ○ tv
- ○ ice
- ○ pull-through
- ○ laundry
- ○ electricity
- ○ 50 amp
- ○ restrooms
- ○ fire ring
- ○ wifi
- ○ cafe
- ○ pool

Activites:

- ○ fishing
- ○ lake
- ○ fitness
- ○ shuffleboard
- ○ hiking
- ○ river
- ○ bike
- ○ pickleball
- ○ canoeing
- ○ hot tub
- ○ boat
- ○ golf

Camped With: _____
_____
_____
_____

New Friends: _____

_____

_____

Places Visited: _____

_____

_____

Drawing / Favorite Photo:

Notes:

_____
_____
_____
_____
_____
_____

Campground: Dates:

Location: _____ Miles: _____

Time: _____ Cost: _____

Travel To Campground: _____ Weather: ☀ ⛅ ⛅ ☁ 🌧 ⛆

INFORMATION:

Name: _____	**Amenities:**
Address: _____	○ easy access ○ picnic table
Phone: _____	○ water ○ tv
Site: _____	○ paved ○ ice
Site For Nest Time: _____	○ 15 amp ○ pull-through
	○ shade ○ laundry
Cost: _____	○ store ○ electricity
Gps: _____	○ firewood ○ 50 amp
Rating: ★ ☆ ☆ ☆ ☆ ☆ ☆	○ security ○ restrooms
Water Pressure: ★ ☆ ☆ ☆ ☆ ☆	○ back-in ○ fire ring
Cleanliness: ★ ☆ ☆ ☆ ☆ ☆ ☆	○ pet friendly ○ wifi
Restrooms: ★ ☆ ☆ ☆ ☆ ☆ ☆	○ sewer ○ cafe
	○ 30 amp ○ pool

Activites:

○ fishing	○ hiking	○ canoeing
○ lake	○ river	○ hot tub
○ fitness	○ bike	○ boat
○ shuffleboard	○ pickleball	○ golf

Camped With: _____

_____

_____

New Friends: _____

_____

_____

Places Visited: _____

_____

_____

Drawing / Favorite Photo:

Notes:

_____
_____
_____
_____
_____
_____

Campground: _____ Dates: _____

Location: _____ Miles: _____
Time: _____ Cost: _____
Travel To Campground: _____ Weather: ☀ ⛅ ☁ 🌧 ⛈

INFORMATION:

Name: _____
Address: _____
Phone: _____
Site: _____
Site For Nest Time: _____
Cost: _____
Gps: _____
Rating: ★ ☆ ☆ ☆ ☆ ☆ ☆
Water Pressure: ★ ☆ ☆ ☆ ☆ ☆
Cleanliness: ★ ☆ ☆ ☆ ☆ ☆ ☆
Restrooms: ★ ☆ ☆ ☆ ☆ ☆ ☆

Amenities:
- ○ easy access
- ○ water
- ○ paved
- ○ 15 amp
- ○ shade
- ○ store
- ○ firewood
- ○ security
- ○ back-in
- ○ pet friendly
- ○ sewer
- ○ 30 amp
- ○ picnic table
- ○ tv
- ○ ice
- ○ pull-through
- ○ laundry
- ○ electricity
- ○ 50 amp
- ○ restrooms
- ○ fire ring
- ○ wifi
- ○ cafe
- ○ pool

Activites:
- ○ fishing
- ○ lake
- ○ fitness
- ○ shuffleboard
- ○ hiking
- ○ river
- ○ bike
- ○ pickleball
- ○ canoeing
- ○ hot tub
- ○ boat
- ○ golf

Camped With: _____
_____
_____

New Friends: _____
_____
_____

Places Visited: _____
_____
_____

Drawing / Favorite Photo:

Notes:
_____
_____
_____
_____
_____
_____

Campground: _____ Dates: _____

Location: _____ Miles: _____
Time: _____ Cost: _____
Travel To Campground: _____ Weather: ☀ ⛅ ☁ 🌧 ⛈

INFORMATION:

Name: _____
Address: _____
Phone: _____
Site: _____
Site For Nest Time: _____
Cost: _____
Gps: _____
Rating: ★ ☆ ☆ ☆ ☆ ☆ ☆
Water Pressure: ★ ☆ ☆ ☆ ☆ ☆
Cleanliness: ★ ☆ ☆ ☆ ☆ ☆ ☆
Restrooms: ★ ☆ ☆ ☆ ☆ ☆ ☆

Amenities:
- ○ easy access
- ○ water
- ○ paved
- ○ 15 amp
- ○ shade
- ○ store
- ○ firewood
- ○ security
- ○ back-in
- ○ pet friendly
- ○ sewer
- ○ 30 amp
- ○ picnic table
- ○ tv
- ○ ice
- ○ pull-through
- ○ laundry
- ○ electricity
- ○ 50 amp
- ○ restrooms
- ○ fire ring
- ○ wifi
- ○ cafe
- ○ pool

Activites:

- ○ fishing
- ○ lake
- ○ fitness
- ○ shuffleboard
- ○ hiking
- ○ river
- ○ bike
- ○ pickleball
- ○ canoeing
- ○ hot tub
- ○ boat
- ○ golf

Camped With: _____
_____
_____
_____

New Friends: _____

_____
_____

Places Visited: _____

_____
_____

Drawing / Favorite Photo:

Notes:
_____
_____
_____
_____
_____

Campground: _____   Dates: _____

Location: _____   Miles: _____

Time: _____   Cost: _____

Travel To Campground: _____   Weather: ☀ ⛅ ⛅ ☁ 🌧

INFORMATION:

Name: _____	**Amenities:**
Address: _____	○ easy access ○ picnic table
Phone: _____	○ water ○ tv
Site: _____	○ paved ○ ice
Site For Nest Time: _____	○ 15 amp ○ pull-through
Cost: _____	○ shade ○ laundry
Gps: _____	○ store ○ electricity
Rating: ★ ☆ ☆ ☆ ☆ ☆ ☆	○ firewood ○ 50 amp
Water Pressure: ★ ☆ ☆ ☆ ☆ ☆	○ security ○ restrooms
Cleanliness: ★ ☆ ☆ ☆ ☆ ☆ ☆	○ back-in ○ fire ring
Restrooms: ★ ☆ ☆ ☆ ☆ ☆ ☆	○ pet friendly ○ wifi
	○ sewer ○ cafe
	○ 30 amp ○ pool

Activites:

○ fishing	○ hiking	○ canoeing
○ lake	○ river	○ hot tub
○ fitness	○ bike	○ boat
○ shuffleboard	○ pickleball	○ golf

Camped With: _____
_____
_____

New Friends: _____

_____

_____

Places Visited: _____

_____

_____

Drawing / Favorite Photo:

Notes:

_____
_____
_____
_____
_____

Campground: Dates:

Location: _____   Miles: _____
Time: _____   Cost: _____
Travel To Campground: _____   Weather: ☀ ⛅ ⛅ ☁ 🌧

INFORMATION:

Name: _____	**Amenities:**
Address: _____	○ easy access ○ picnic table
Phone: _____	○ water ○ tv
Site: _____	○ paved ○ ice
Site For Nest Time: _____	○ 15 amp ○ pull-through
Cost: _____	○ shade ○ laundry
Gps: _____	○ store ○ electricity
Rating: ★ ☆ ☆ ☆ ☆ ☆ ☆	○ firewood ○ 50 amp
Water Pressure: ★ ☆ ☆ ☆ ☆ ☆	○ security ○ restrooms
Cleanliness: ★ ☆ ☆ ☆ ☆ ☆ ☆	○ back-in ○ fire ring
Restrooms: ★ ☆ ☆ ☆ ☆ ☆ ☆	○ pet friendly ○ wifi
	○ sewer ○ cafe
	○ 30 amp ○ pool

Activites:

○ fishing	○ hiking	○ canoeing
○ lake	○ river	○ hot tub
○ fitness	○ bike	○ boat
○ shuffleboard	○ pickleball	○ golf

Camped With: _____
_____
_____

New Friends: _____

_____
_____

Places Visited: _____

_____
_____

Drawing / Favorite Photo:

Notes:

Campground: # Dates:

Location: _____ Miles: _____

Time: _____ Cost: _____

Travel To Campground: _____ Weather: ☀ ⛅ ☁ 🌧 ⛈

INFORMATION:

Name: _____	**Amenities:**
Address: _____	○ easy access ○ picnic table
Phone: _____	○ water ○ tv
Site: _____	○ paved ○ ice
Site For Nest Time: _____	○ 15 amp ○ pull-through
Cost: _____	○ shade ○ laundry
Gps: _____	○ store ○ electricity
Rating: ★ ☆ ☆ ☆ ☆ ☆ ☆	○ firewood ○ 50 amp
Water Pressure: ★ ☆ ☆ ☆ ☆ ☆	○ security ○ restrooms
Cleanliness: ★ ☆ ☆ ☆ ☆ ☆ ☆	○ back-in ○ fire ring
Restrooms: ★ ☆ ☆ ☆ ☆ ☆ ☆	○ pet friendly ○ wifi
	○ sewer ○ cafe
	○ 30 amp ○ pool

Activites:

○ fishing	○ hiking	○ canoeing
○ lake	○ river	○ hot tub
○ fitness	○ bike	○ boat
○ shuffleboard	○ pickleball	○ golf

Camped With: _____
_____
_____

New Friends: _____

_____
_____

Places Visited: _____

_____
_____

Drawing / Favorite Photo:

Notes:

Campground: Dates:

Location: _____   Miles: _____

Time: _____   Cost: _____

Travel To Campground: _____   Weather: ☀ ⛅ ☁ 🌧 ⛈

INFORMATION:

Name: _____

Address: _____

Phone: _____

Site: _____

Site For Nest Time: _____

Cost: _____

Gps: _____

Rating: ★ ☆ ☆ ☆ ☆ ☆ ☆

Water Pressure: ★ ☆ ☆ ☆ ☆

Cleanliness: ★ ☆ ☆ ☆ ☆ ☆

Restrooms: ★ ☆ ☆ ☆ ☆ ☆

Amenities:

- ○ easy access
- ○ water
- ○ paved
- ○ 15 amp
- ○ shade
- ○ store
- ○ firewood
- ○ security
- ○ back-in
- ○ pet friendly
- ○ sewer
- ○ 30 amp

- ○ picnic table
- ○ tv
- ○ ice
- ○ pull-through
- ○ laundry
- ○ electricity
- ○ 50 amp
- ○ restrooms
- ○ fire ring
- ○ wifi
- ○ cafe
- ○ pool

Activites:

- ○ fishing
- ○ lake
- ○ fitness
- ○ shuffleboard

- ○ hiking
- ○ river
- ○ bike
- ○ pickleball

- ○ canoeing
- ○ hot tub
- ○ boat
- ○ golf

Camped With: _____

_____

_____

New Friends: _____
_____
_____

Places Visited: _____
_____
_____

Drawing / Favorite Photo:

Notes:
_____
_____
_____
_____
_____

Campground: Dates:

Location: _____ Miles: _____

Time: _____ Cost: _____

Travel To Campground: _____ Weather: ☀ ⛅ ☁ 🌧 ⛈

INFORMATION:

Name: _____	Amenities:
Address: _____	○ easy access ○ picnic table
Phone: _____	○ water ○ tv
Site: _____	○ paved ○ ice
Site For Nest Time: _____	○ 15 amp ○ pull-through
	○ shade ○ laundry
Cost: _____	○ store ○ electricity
Gps: _____	○ firewood ○ 50 amp
Rating: ★ ☆ ☆ ☆ ☆ ☆ ☆	○ security ○ restrooms
Water Pressure: ★ ☆ ☆ ☆ ☆ ☆	○ back-in ○ fire ring
Cleanliness: ★ ☆ ☆ ☆ ☆ ☆ ☆	○ pet friendly ○ wifi
	○ sewer ○ cafe
Restrooms: ★ ☆ ☆ ☆ ☆ ☆ ☆	○ 30 amp ○ pool

Activites:

○ fishing	○ hiking	○ canoeing
○ lake	○ river	○ hot tub
○ fitness	○ bike	○ boat
○ shuffleboard	○ pickleball	○ golf

Camped With: _____

_____

_____

New Friends: _____
_____
_____

Places Visited: _____
_____
_____

Drawing / Favorite Photo:

Notes:
_____
_____
_____
_____
_____

Campground: Dates:

Location: _____ Miles: _____
Time: _____ Cost: _____
Travel To Campground: _____ Weather: ☀ ⛅ ☁ 🌧 ⛈

INFORMATION:

	Amenities:	
Name: _____	○ easy access	○ picnic table
Address: _____	○ water	○ tv
Phone: _____	○ paved	○ ice
Site: _____	○ 15 amp	○ pull-through
Site For Nest Time: _____	○ shade	○ laundry
Cost: _____	○ store	○ electricity
Gps: _____	○ firewood	○ 50 amp
Rating: ★ ☆ ☆ ☆ ☆ ☆ ☆	○ security	○ restrooms
Water Pressure: ★ ☆ ☆ ☆ ☆ ☆	○ back-in	○ fire ring
Cleanliness: ★ ☆ ☆ ☆ ☆ ☆	○ pet friendly	○ wifi
Restrooms: ★ ☆ ☆ ☆ ☆ ☆	○ sewer	○ cafe
	○ 30 amp	○ pool

Activites:

○ fishing	○ hiking	○ canoeing
○ lake	○ river	○ hot tub
○ fitness	○ bike	○ boat
○ shuffleboard	○ pickleball	○ golf

Camped With: _____
_____
_____
_____

New Friends: _____
_____
_____

Places Visited: _____
_____
_____

Drawing / Favorite Photo:

Notes:
_____
_____
_____
_____
_____

Campground: _____   Dates: _____

Location: _____   Miles: _____
Time: _____   Cost: _____
Travel To Campground: _____   Weather: ☀ ⛅ ⛅ ☁ 🌧

INFORMATION:

Name: _____
Address: _____
Phone: _____
Site: _____
Site For Nest Time: _____
Cost: _____
Gps: _____
Rating: ★ ☆ ☆ ☆ ☆ ☆
Water Pressure: ★ ☆ ☆ ☆ ☆ ☆
Cleanliness: ★ ☆ ☆ ☆ ☆ ☆
Restrooms: ★ ☆ ☆ ☆ ☆ ☆

Amenities:
- ○ easy access   ○ picnic table
- ○ water   ○ tv
- ○ paved   ○ ice
- ○ 15 amp   ○ pull-through
- ○ shade   ○ laundry
- ○ store   ○ electricity
- ○ firewood   ○ 50 amp
- ○ security   ○ restrooms
- ○ back-in   ○ fire ring
- ○ pet friendly   ○ wifi
- ○ sewer   ○ cafe
- ○ 30 amp   ○ pool

Activites:

- ○ fishing   ○ hiking   ○ canoeing
- ○ lake   ○ river   ○ hot tub
- ○ fitness   ○ bike   ○ boat
- ○ shuffleboard   ○ pickleball   ○ golf

Camped With: _____
_____
_____

New Friends: _____

_____

_____

Places Visited: _____

_____

_____

Drawing / Favorite Photo:

Notes:

_____
_____
_____
_____
_____

Campground: Dates:

Location: _____   Miles: _____

Time: _____   Cost: _____

Travel To Campground: _____   Weather: ☀ ⛅ ☁ 🌧 ⛈

INFORMATION:

Name: _____	**Amenities:**
Address: _____	○ easy access ○ picnic table
Phone: _____	○ water ○ tv
Site: _____	○ paved ○ ice
Site For Nest Time: ____	○ 15 amp ○ pull-through
	○ shade ○ laundry
Cost: _____	○ store ○ electricity
Gps: _____	○ firewood ○ 50 amp
Rating: ★ ☆ ☆ ☆ ☆ ☆ ☆	○ security ○ restrooms
Water Pressure: ★ ☆ ☆ ☆ ☆ ☆	○ back-in ○ fire ring
Cleanliness: ★ ☆ ☆ ☆ ☆ ☆ ☆	○ pet friendly ○ wifi
	○ sewer ○ cafe
Restrooms: ★ ☆ ☆ ☆ ☆ ☆ ☆	○ 30 amp ○ pool

Activites:

○ fishing	○ hiking	○ canoeing
○ lake	○ river	○ hot tub
○ fitness	○ bike	○ boat
○ shuffleboard	○ pickleball	○ golf

Camped With: _____

_____

_____

New Friends: _____

_____

_____

Places Visited: _____

_____

_____

Drawing / Favorite Photo:

Notes:

_____
_____
_____
_____
_____

Campground: _____ Dates: _____

Location: _____ Miles: _____

Time: _____ Cost: _____

Travel To Campground: _____ Weather: ☀ ⛅ ⛅ ☁ 🌧 🌨

INFORMATION:

Name: _____	**Amenities:**
Address: _____	○ easy access ○ picnic table
Phone: _____	○ water ○ tv
Site: _____	○ paved ○ ice
Site For Nest Time: _____	○ 15 amp ○ pull-through
Cost: _____	○ shade ○ laundry
Gps: _____	○ store ○ electricity
Rating: ★ ☆ ☆ ☆ ☆ ☆ ☆	○ firewood ○ 50 amp
Water Pressure: ★ ☆ ☆ ☆ ☆ ☆	○ security ○ restrooms
Cleanliness: ★ ☆ ☆ ☆ ☆ ☆ ☆	○ back-in ○ fire ring
Restrooms: ★ ☆ ☆ ☆ ☆ ☆ ☆	○ pet friendly ○ wifi
	○ sewer ○ cafe
	○ 30 amp ○ pool

Activites:

○ fishing	○ hiking	○ canoeing
○ lake	○ river	○ hot tub
○ fitness	○ bike	○ boat
○ shuffleboard	○ pickleball	○ golf

Camped With: _____

_____

_____

New Friends: _____

_____

_____

Places Visited: _____

_____

_____

Drawing / Favorite Photo:

Notes:

Campground:

Dates:

Location: _____ Miles: _____

Time: _____ Cost: _____

Travel To Campground: _____ Weather: ☀ ⛅ ⛅ ☁ 🌧

INFORMATION:

Name: _____

Address: _____

Phone: _____

Site: _____

Site For Nest Time: _____

Cost: _____

Gps: _____

Rating: ★ ☆ ☆ ☆ ☆ ☆ ☆

Water Pressure: ★ ☆ ☆ ☆ ☆ ☆

Cleanliness: ★ ☆ ☆ ☆ ☆ ☆ ☆

Restrooms: ★ ☆ ☆ ☆ ☆ ☆ ☆

Amenities:
- ○ easy access
- ○ water
- ○ paved
- ○ 15 amp
- ○ shade
- ○ store
- ○ firewood
- ○ security
- ○ back-in
- ○ pet friendly
- ○ sewer
- ○ 30 amp
- ○ picnic table
- ○ tv
- ○ ice
- ○ pull-through
- ○ laundry
- ○ electricity
- ○ 50 amp
- ○ restrooms
- ○ fire ring
- ○ wifi
- ○ cafe
- ○ pool

Activites:

- ○ fishing
- ○ lake
- ○ fitness
- ○ shuffleboard
- ○ hiking
- ○ river
- ○ bike
- ○ pickleball
- ○ canoeing
- ○ hot tub
- ○ boat
- ○ golf

Camped With: _____
_____
_____
_____

New Friends: _____

_____

_____

Places Visited: _____

_____

_____

Drawing / Favorite Photo:

Notes:
_____
_____
_____
_____
_____

Campground: Dates:

Location: _____   Miles: _____
Time: _____   Cost: _____
Travel To Campground: _____ Weather: ☼ ⛅ ☁ 🌧 ⛈

INFORMATION:

Name: _____	Amenities:
Address: _____	○ easy access ○ picnic table
Phone: _____	○ water ○ tv
Site: _____	○ paved ○ ice
Site For Nest Time: _____	○ 15 amp ○ pull-through
Cost: _____	○ shade ○ laundry
Gps: _____	○ store ○ electricity
Rating: ★ ☆ ☆ ☆ ☆ ☆ ☆	○ firewood ○ 50 amp
Water Pressure: ★ ☆ ☆ ☆ ☆ ☆	○ security ○ restrooms
Cleanliness: ★ ☆ ☆ ☆ ☆ ☆ ☆	○ back-in ○ fire ring
Restrooms: ★ ☆ ☆ ☆ ☆ ☆ ☆	○ pet friendly ○ wifi
	○ sewer ○ cafe
	○ 30 amp ○ pool

Activites:

○ fishing   ○ hiking   ○ canoeing
○ lake   ○ river   ○ hot tub
○ fitness   ○ bike   ○ boat
○ shuffleboard   ○ pickleball   ○ golf

Camped With: _____
_____
_____

New Friends: _____

_____

_____

Places Visited: _____

_____

_____

Drawing / Favorite Photo:

Notes:

_____
_____
_____
_____
_____
_____

Campground: Dates:

Location: _____   Miles: _____
Time: _____   Cost: _____
Travel To Campground: _____   Weather: ☀ ⛅ ☁ 🌧 ⛈

INFORMATION:

Name: _____	**Amenities:**
Address: _____	○ easy access ○ picnic table
Phone: _____	○ water ○ tv
Site: _____	○ paved ○ ice
Site For Nest Time: _____	○ 15 amp ○ pull-through
Cost: _____	○ shade ○ laundry
Gps: _____	○ store ○ electricity
Rating: ★ ☆ ☆ ☆ ☆ ☆ ☆	○ firewood ○ 50 amp
Water Pressure: ★ ☆ ☆ ☆ ☆ ☆	○ security ○ restrooms
Cleanliness: ★ ☆ ☆ ☆ ☆ ☆ ☆	○ back-in ○ fire ring
Restrooms: ★ ☆ ☆ ☆ ☆ ☆ ☆	○ pet friendly ○ wifi
	○ sewer ○ cafe
	○ 30 amp ○ pool

Activites:

○ fishing   ○ hiking   ○ canoeing
○ lake   ○ river   ○ hot tub
○ fitness   ○ bike   ○ boat
○ shuffleboard   ○ pickleball   ○ golf

Camped With: _____
_____
_____

New Friends: _____

_____

_____

Places Visited: _____

_____

_____

Drawing / Favorite Photo:

Notes:

Campground:

Dates:

Location: _____ Miles: _____

Time: _____ Cost: _____

Travel To Campground: _____ Weather: ☀ 🌤 ⛅ 🌧 ⛈

INFORMATION:

Name: _____

Address: _____

Phone: _____

Site: _____

Site For Nest Time: _____

Cost: _____

Gps: _____

Rating: ★ ☆ ☆ ☆ ☆ ☆ ☆

Water Pressure: ★ ☆ ☆ ☆ ☆ ☆

Cleanliness: ★ ☆ ☆ ☆ ☆ ☆ ☆

Restrooms: ★ ☆ ☆ ☆ ☆ ☆ ☆

Amenities:

- ○ easy access
- ○ water
- ○ paved
- ○ 15 amp
- ○ shade
- ○ store
- ○ firewood
- ○ security
- ○ back-in
- ○ pet friendly
- ○ sewer
- ○ 30 amp
- ○ picnic table
- ○ tv
- ○ ice
- ○ pull-through
- ○ laundry
- ○ electricity
- ○ 50 amp
- ○ restrooms
- ○ fire ring
- ○ wifi
- ○ cafe
- ○ pool

Activites:

- ○ fishing
- ○ lake
- ○ fitness
- ○ shuffleboard
- ○ hiking
- ○ river
- ○ bike
- ○ pickleball
- ○ canoeing
- ○ hot tub
- ○ boat
- ○ golf

Camped With: _____

_____

_____

New Friends: _____

_____

_____

Places Visited: _____

_____

_____

Drawing / Favorite Photo:

Notes:

Campground: _____   Dates: _____

Location: _____   Miles: _____

Time: _____   Cost: _____

Travel To Campground: _____   Weather: ☀ ⛅ ☁ 🌧 ⛈

INFORMATION:

Name: _____	**Amenities:**
Address: _____	○ easy access ○ picnic table
Phone: _____	○ water ○ tv
Site: _____	○ paved ○ ice
Site For Nest Time: _____	○ 15 amp ○ pull-through
Cost: _____	○ shade ○ laundry
Gps: _____	○ store ○ electricity
Rating: ★ ☆ ☆ ☆ ☆ ☆ ☆	○ firewood ○ 50 amp
Water Pressure: ★ ☆ ☆ ☆ ☆	○ security ○ restrooms
Cleanliness: ★ ☆ ☆ ☆ ☆ ☆	○ back-in ○ fire ring
Restrooms: ★ ☆ ☆ ☆ ☆ ☆	○ pet friendly ○ wifi
	○ sewer ○ cafe
	○ 30 amp ○ pool

Activites:

○ fishing   ○ hiking   ○ canoeing
○ lake   ○ river   ○ hot tub
○ fitness   ○ bike   ○ boat
○ shuffleboard   ○ pickleball   ○ golf

Camped With: _____
_____
_____

New Friends: _____

Places Visited: _____

Drawing / Favorite Photo:

Notes:

Campground: Dates:

Location: _____   Miles: _____

Time: _____   Cost: _____

Travel To Campground: _____   Weather: ☀ ⛅ ☁ 🌧 ⛈

INFORMATION:

Name: _____

Address: _____

Phone: _____

Site: _____

Site For Nest Time: _____

Cost: _____

Gps: _____

Rating: ★ ☆ ☆ ☆ ☆ ☆ ☆

Water Pressure: ★ ☆ ☆ ☆ ☆ ☆

Cleanliness: ★ ☆ ☆ ☆ ☆ ☆ ☆

Restrooms: ★ ☆ ☆ ☆ ☆ ☆ ☆

Amenities:

- ○ easy access
- ○ water
- ○ paved
- ○ 15 amp
- ○ shade
- ○ store
- ○ firewood
- ○ security
- ○ back-in
- ○ pet friendly
- ○ sewer
- ○ 30 amp
- ○ picnic table
- ○ tv
- ○ ice
- ○ pull-through
- ○ laundry
- ○ electricity
- ○ 50 amp
- ○ restrooms
- ○ fire ring
- ○ wifi
- ○ cafe
- ○ pool

Activites:

- ○ fishing
- ○ lake
- ○ fitness
- ○ shuffleboard
- ○ hiking
- ○ river
- ○ bike
- ○ pickleball
- ○ canoeing
- ○ hot tub
- ○ boat
- ○ golf

Camped With: _____

_____

_____

Printed by Amazon Italia Logistica S.r.l.
Torrazza Piemonte (TO), Italy

39546008R00058